# Indians of the Northwest Coast

## Preface

Of all the Native American culture areas, the Northwest Coast, from Southern Alaska to Puget Sound, was the wealthiest. The Northwest natives did everything in a big way. The Indians of the Northwest had the largest population. Their homes were big. They built giant totem poles. They traveled in large dugout canoes. Their arts and crafts were elaborate. They gave huge parties. Nature provided all the necessary resources. The natives developed practical and efficient ways to use them.

By the time the Northwest Coast Indians came in contact with Europeans, other areas had already been explored, and the natives had already been labeled "Indians." The term is used in this book only to identify them as the group of natives who first inhabited the Northwest Coast of America.

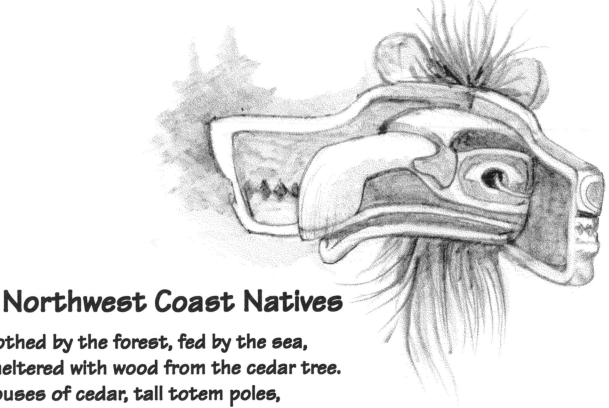

## Northwest Coast Natives

Clothed by the forest, fed by the sea,
Sheltered with wood from the cedar tree.
Houses of cedar, tall totem poles,
Cedar wood carved into boxes and bowls.

Dugout canoes gigantic in size,
Carried hunters pursuing the whale, a great prize.

Potlashes lavish, pretentious and gay...
Stores of one's riches given away.
Chiefs and nobles, workers and slaves...
Backs to the mountains, facing the waves.

—by Elaine Cleary

# Bibliography

## Resource Books for Teachers

*America's Fascinating Indian Heritage* by James A. Maxwell, Ed; Reader's Digest, 1992.

*The American Indian* by Anne Terry White; Random House, 1963.

*Atlas of the North American Indian* by Carl Waldman; Facts on File Publication, 1985.

*Children of the Raven* by H.R. Hays; McGraw-Hill, 1975.

*The First Americans* by Editors of Time-Life Books; The Time, Inc. Book Co.,1992.

*Lost Heritage of Alaska* by Polly Miller; World Publishing Co., 1967.

*North American Indians* by Alice B. Kehoe; Prentice-Hall, 1981.

*The Totem Pole Indians* by Joseph H. Wherry; Wilfred Funk, Inc., 1964.

*Winter Brothers* by Ivan Doig; Harcourt Brace Jovanovich, 1980.

## Books for Intermediate Readers

*From Abenaki to Zuni* by Evelyn Wolfson; Walker & Co., 1988.

*How Indians Really Lived* by Gordon C. Baldwin; G.P. Putnam's Sons, 1967.

*Indian Costumes* by Robert Hofsinde (Gray Wolf); William Morrow & Co., 1968.

*Indian Hunting* by Robert Hofsinde (Gray Wolf); William Morrow & Co., 1962.

*Native American Animal Stories* by Joseph Bruchac; Fulcrum Publishing, 1992.

*Native American Stories* by Joseph Bruchac; Fulcrum Publishing, 1991.

*Once Upon a Totem* by Christie Harris; Atheneum, 1963.

Note: This activity may be done as a whole-group brainstorming session or in cooperative learning groups. Combine all information to create a large chart to leave up in class throughout the unit of study.

# Before We Begin

| What we know about *Northwest Coast Indians* | What we want to learn about *Northwest Coast Indians* |
| --- | --- |
| | |

# History

Scientists believe the natives of the Northwest coast came to this continent from Asia many thousands of years ago, entering Alaska over a land mass that is now covered by the Bering Strait. While earlier groups continued on far to the south and east, this group stayed along the coast from what is now Alaska to Northern California.

Long, long ago they probably lived in pole homes covered with skins and slabs of bark. Fishing was probably done from skin boats that stayed close to shore, or from the shore itself.

When the sea level stabilized, about 5,000 years ago, it became possible to establish small settlements closer to shore. The people could now turn from the thick forests to the sea for food. Fish and sea mammals provided a constant food supply, rich in protein and easy to obtain. Tools designed for very special purposes have been found indicating that these natives were becoming skilled workers at this time.

As their methods of getting and preserving food improved, the population grew. Larger villages were built. People had more time to spend on art, crafts, and other leisure-time activities. Those who accumulated the most food and wealth became leaders, and clans and tribes were established.

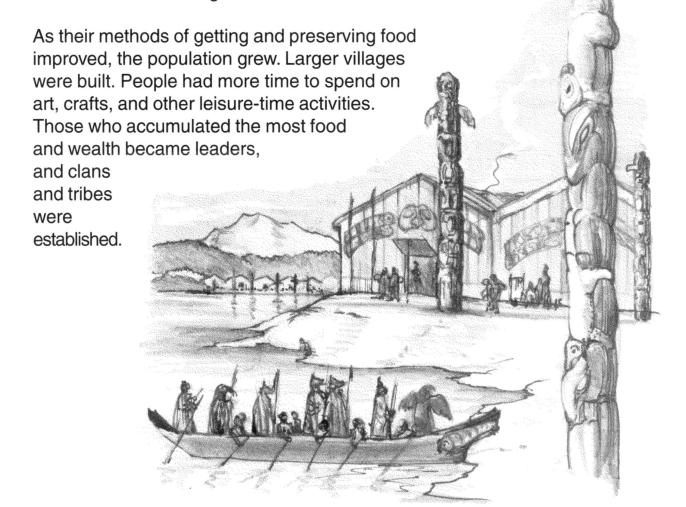

# Geography

The Northwest coastal area is a maritime region controlled by the sea. It is a narrow strip of land 1,000 miles long extending from southern Alaska to Puget Sound and includes thousands of islands. To the west is the Pacific Ocean. To the east are the steep forest-covered Coast Mountains, and the Cascade Range extends to the south. There are two main rivers, the Fraser and the Columbia. The Japan current flowing along southern Alaska and down the shoreline keeps the climate moderate. Its warm moist air is stopped by the mountains, causing misty rain to fall on the slopes. Summers are cool. Winters are wet.

**Map Activity:**
Have the class make a large map of the area inhabited by the Northwest Coast Indians.

**Materials:**
- large sheets of bulletin board paper taped or glued together to be 10' x 10' (3m x 3m)
- yard stick/metric stick
- copies of the grid map on the next page

**Directions:**
1. Divide the bulletin board paper into 6" (15 cm) squares.
2. Number the squares 1—20 vertically and A—T horizontally.
3. Give students copies of the grid map on the next page.
4. Assign small groups to enlarge the map one square at a time by drawing matching lines in corresponding squares. Assign each group specific grid squares.
5. Using an atlas find, draw, and label on the big map:

| | | |
|---|---|---|
| Alaska | Queen Charlotte Islands | Canada |
| Pacific Ocean | Puget Sound | United States |
| Fraser River | Columbia River | Bering Strait |
| Coast Mountains | Cascade Range | Vancouver Island |

Note: Once the large map is drawn, it can be laminated and labelled with washable pens. This way it can be wiped clean and used over again for other activities.

# Grid Map of North America

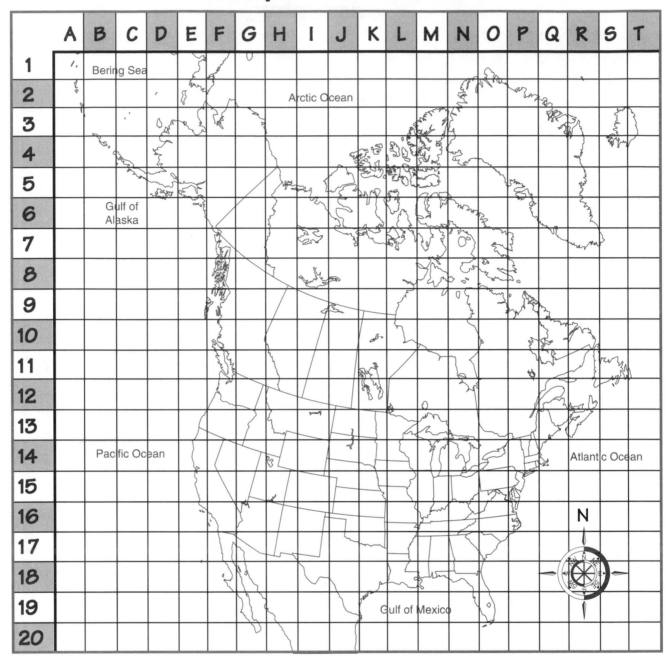

You can locate where some of the Northwest Coast tribes lived by using your grid.

| Squares: | Tribe: |
|----------|--------|
| 7F, 8F | Tlingit |
| 9E | Haida (island) |
| 9F | Tsimshian |
| 10F | Bella Bella  (northeast corner) |
| 10F | Kwakiutl  (southwest corner) |
| 10F, 11F | Nootka (island) |
| 11E, 11F | Makah |

Northwest Indians EMC 557

# 3-D Geography

Your students can show the Northwest Coast's beautiful scenery by making a 3-D picture.

**Materials:**
- 9" x 12" (23 cm x 30.5 cm) sheet of light blue construction paper
- 9" x 4" (23 cm x 10 cm) sheet of green construction paper
- crayons, markers or tempera paints
- scissors and glue
- scraps of construction paper

**Directions:**
1. Fold your blue paper in half width-wise.
2. Place half of the blue paper on the desk (A). Bend half to stand upright (B).
3. Divide the flat section by drawing a light pencil line 4" (10 cm) from the edge (C).
4. On section B draw jagged mountains with snow-capped peaks.
   Color them in shades of purple.
5. Fold 1" (2.5 cm) under along the 9" (23 cm) edge of your green paper.
6. Using the folded edge as the bottom, draw cedar trees shaped like tall thin triangles in the top 3" (7.5 cm) space.
7. Draw straight brownish-black trunks on the trees.
8. Trim the top points of the trees with scissors.
9. Stand this section by gluing the 1" (2.5 cm) strip along the pencil line (C).
10. Use the front 4" (10 cm) of the blue paper for the sea and shore.
11. Draw waves on the blue for the water.
12. Color the shoreline light brown.
13. You can add canoes to the water and houses to the shore by cutting them out of scrap paper, folding under a tab on the bottom, and gluing them in place.

 Northwest Indians EMC 557

# Increase Your Geography Vocabulary

The words below are all connected in some way to the geography of the Northwest Coast. Look them up in a dictionary.

Underline those associated with water. Circle those associated with land.

| | | | |
|---|---|---|---|
| archipelago | bay | bluff | coast |
| estuary | fiord | sea | gulf |
| strait | island | lagoon | inland waterway |
| midden | mouth | peninsula | range |
| plain | ridge | sound | tundra |

Using a map of North America, find examples of five land forms and five water forms. Write their names and type of form below.

| Land Forms | | Water Forms | |
|---|---|---|---|
| Name | Type of form | Name | Type of form |
| 1. _____ | | 1. _____ | |
| 2. _____ | | 2. _____ | |
| 3. _____ | | 3. _____ | |
| 4. _____ | | 4. _____ | |
| 5. _____ | | 5. _____ | |

Are there any of these in the area in which you live?
Have you ever traveled to an area where they are?

# Which Means Which?

Each of the following words has two definitions, one of which is geographical. Use a dictionary to find both meanings. Then write one sentence using the word both ways.

> **Example:**
>
> word - **bluff**
>     (1) to mislead
>     (2) high, steep riverbed
> sentence - He bluffed the enemy into thinking there was a bluff nearby.

word - **bay**
    (1) _____
    (2) _____
sentence - _____ .

word - **coast**
    (1) _____
    (2) _____
sentence - _____ .

word - **mouth**
    (1) _____
    (2) _____
sentence - _____ .

word - **range**
    (1) _____
    (2 _____
sentence - _____ .

word - **sound**
    (1) _____
    (2) _____
sentence - _____ .

word - **plain**
    (1) _____
    (2) _____
sentence - _____

# Social Structure

Unlike other native groups in America, those on the Northwest Coast did not practice democracy. A person's worth or class depended upon his wealth, and his wealth came from his property and titles. The class a person was born into was the class he stayed in for life.

Highest ranking were the chiefs, or house owners. The richest chief was the most powerful and, therefore, the village chief. His closest family members were next highest. These people made up the "noble" class.

Next came the "commoners." These included the rest of the village, the working class. Even here some were higher than others. For example, skilled craftsmen (such as canoe makers and totem pole carvers) or brave warriors ranked above fishermen or weavers.

Then there were the slaves. Traded for or captured in raids, all wealthy families owned them. Some slaves added to their owners' wealth by the work they did—weaving, hunting, fishing, and carving. Others helped with household chores. A slave had no rights. He could be bought, sold, given away or killed at the owner's will. Owners could give slaves their freedom, but this rarely happened. Slavery was an accepted part of Northwest society.

# "Money" and Trade

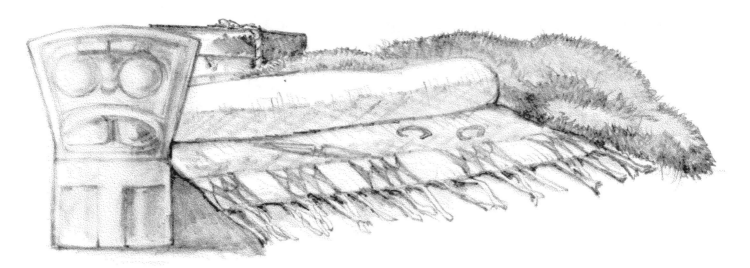

Wealth was all-important. A man kept his social position by accumulating things, showing off his wealth, and finally giving it away—only to accumulate more all over again. Because the Indians of the Northwest coast owned more than they needed, they used the surplus to trade or buy other things.

One thing used as "money" by all Pacific Coast Indians was a kind of shiny white shell called dentalium. Another was blankets woven from the wool of mountain goats. The goats were hard to hunt, and the blankets took many hours to weave, thus making them valuable. These blankets were collected and saved, just as other people saved money, and then used to buy expensive items such as slaves or canoes.

"Coppers" were another medium of exchange. Considered the greatest example of wealth, they were shields, about 3 feet high with the top half elaborately engraved. Other indications of wealth were canoes, masks, sea otter and ermine skins, and slaves. Some of the items sought in trade were seal skins, mountain goat horns, whale bones, oil, raw copper, sea-going canoes, and Chilkat blankets.

Other things thought of as wealth were inherited from one generation to another. For example, special fishing or berry-picking areas, the right to sing a certain song or do a special dance, the use of a particular crest, and the right to certain titles, were thought of as wealth.

# Homes

Early Northwest Natives built pit-house-style homes. These were abandoned when tools, such as adzes and wedges, were developed. With tools, tall cedar trees could be split into planks big enough to build houses that could accommodate large families. The houses were built in rows, usually along a sandy beach.

Homes varied somewhat from tribe to tribe, but all were frame buildings made of log posts covered with cedar or spruce boards. Smaller logs supported the roof shingles. These shingles, held down with rocks, could be moved easily by poles to let out smoke or to let in fresh air.

There were no windows; smoke holes were the only permanent vents. The doorway of some homes was an opening cut through a large, intricately-carved pole in the center of the front wall. Floors were made of dirt or cedar planks, with one common fire pit in the center. The whole household used that fire for both heat and cooking. Around it was a wide raised platform off which were the sleeping compartments. The place of honor, directly across from the outside doorway, was reserved for the house chief. Next to him were the compartments of the next highest ranking families and so on to the back of the house, where the servants or slaves were quartered.

# Make a Northwest Coast Village

Students will enjoy creating a village of cedar plank houses.

**Materials each student will need:**
- shoe box (lid not necessary)
- piece of cardboard a little longer and wider than the top of the shoe box
- cardboard tube from paper towel roll
- gray construction paper
- crayons, markers or tempera paint
- glue
- small stones

**Directions:**
1. Tear strips of gray paper about 1" (2.5 cm) wide.
2. Glue them vertically to all four sides of the shoe box.
3. Shade in the grain of the wood.
4. Cut the cardboard tube 3" (7.5 cm) higher than the front wall.
5. Cover it with gray paper.
6. Decorate with animal designs.
7. Cut an oval 2" (5 cm) high up the bottom of the tube for an entrance.
8. Glue the roll vertically to the center of the front wall.
9. Fold cardboard lengthwise for the roof.
10. Glue torn construction paper overlapping horizontally on the roof.
11. Cut a smoke hole in the center.
12. Glue or tape the roof to the walls.
13. Glue stones to the roof.

Arrange the homes in a line along a shore of blue paper and brown sand.
A background of green cedar trees and paper canoes on the beach can be added.

# Cedar, the Indispensable

While sea and stream provided most of the food for the Northwest Indians, the thick forests provided most of their clothing, shelter, and material for much of their arts and crafts. Of all the trees, the most valuable was the cedar.

Trunks were used for houseposts. Hollowed-out logs were used for canoes. Masks and figures were carved, as were bowls and utensils. The coarse outer bark was woven into storage baskets, screens, and sleeping mats. The softer inner bark was made into fine fibers to weave tablecloths, cone-shaped hats, skirts, capes, and ponchos. Cradles were padded with the soft fibers, babies diapered and wrapped in it.

Because the cedar tree has a fine, straight grain it can be split into boards, used to make boxes, bows, arrows, spears, and clubs.

Tree roots were used for cord, rope, and basket-making.

Wooden slats were sewn together and used as armor when worn over tough hide vests.

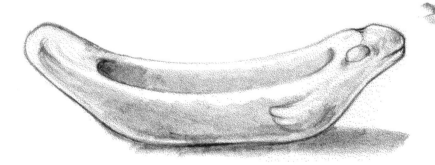

# Cedar, the Tree of Many Uses

Use the word box to find some of the many uses for cedar that are hidden in the word search.

| | | | |
|---|---|---|---|
| arrow | basket | blanket | board |
| bow | box | canoe | cape |
| club | container | cord | diaper |
| firewood | hat | housepost | mask |
| mat | poncho | roof | rope |
| screen | skirt | spear | tinder |

## Cedar Search

```
A C R W I J K N M S B T
B Y T I N D E R M A A L
S P E A R Q R H A T S A
H O U S E P O S T E K K
O N S C A N O E E R E J
F C C O A B F X J S T M
I H O N B P N B O W E A
R O R T A L E C D E I K
E D D A S I A B H B K A
W S K I R T C N L O I R
O C E N A O D N K X S R
O R O E F P H C M E J O
D E G R O P E P L M T W
Y E R W D I R R L U B T
N N A N O B O A R D B M
```

# Cedar, Cedar, Cedar

All North American natives were conscious of using resources wisely. The Northwest Coast Indians were no exception. When they only needed to use the bark, they stripped just as much as necessary without killing the tree. When a cedar tree fell, they used all the parts.

Using the words from the Cedar Search on page 15 and the information on page 14, fill in the chart below to show what part of the cedar tree was used to make each of the items.

| trunk | outer bark | inner bark | roots | branches |
|-------|-----------|-----------|-------|----------|
|       |           |           |       |          |

# Clothing

In warm weather, Northwest Coast Indian men wore very little except a woven hat with a broad brim to protect their eyes from the sun's glare on the water. When it rained they put on ponchos woven from shredded cedar bark that had been oiled to make it waterproof and rain hats woven from spruce roots.

Women wore skirts, tunics, or sarongs sometimes made of deerskin, but usually woven from cedar bark. Weaving material was made from the soft inner bark of the cedar tree. This was soaked until soft, beaten until it broke into soft shreds, then rolled between the palm and the thigh until they were just the right thickness for weaving. Threads were woven so tightly that they were waterproof. Fur, bird's down, or goat hair was put around the neck to make it soft.

In very cold weather, men wore seal or deerskin leggings and moccasins, and they wrapped themselves in cedar bark robes that came up over their heads. Women kept warm in cedar bark robes that had elbow-length sleeves. In extremely cold weather, both men and women wrapped themselves in furs.

Headpieces worn by chiefs were carved from wood and decorated with shells, ermine tails, and sea lion whiskers.

Men and women wore copper bracelets, anklets, necklaces, and headbands. Noses, as well as ears, were pierced to wear ornaments of bone, shell, wood, copper, or feathers.

To protect their skin from weather and insects, they painted their faces with bear grease or fish oil mixed with black or red ocher. This same mixture was rubbed into their hair, giving it a shiny, greased look that they considered beautiful.

Facial tattooing was another status mark. Many natives had family crests tattooed and men, especially, had animal designs tattooed all over their bodies.

Unlike other native groups, Northwest Coastal men had much facial hair. They wore heavy mustaches and often grew beards. Their hair was worn shoulder length. Women wore their hair in thick braids.

# Clothing

Much of the clothing worn by the Northwest Coast natives was unique to them. How strange they must have appeared to the first Europeans! The Europeans must have also given a strange impression to the natives. Think how both of those groups would react to the clothing we wear today!

Using what you know and books and materials available to you, compare the style of clothing of these three groups by filling in the chart below.

| | Northwest Coast Natives | First Europeans in North America | Present-day Americans |
|---|---|---|---|
| **footwear** | | | |
| **headwear** | | | |
| **shirts** | | | |
| **skirts** | | | |
| **pants** | | | |
| **outerwear** | | | |
| **rainwear** | | | |
| **armor** | | | |

# Chilkat Blankets

Tlingit and Tsimshian women wove goat's hair with cedar bark to make beautiful blankets worn only by chiefs or persons of high rank.

Designs represented parts of fish, birds or animals. The blanket was woven in shades of yellow, blue, black and the natural off-white wool color, and trimmed with long fringe at the bottom. Divided down the middle, the pattern is repeated from one side to the other as a mirror image.

It took a year to design the pattern; make, dye, and dry the yarn; and do the actual weaving. Chilkat blankets were valued for their beauty, and other tribes eagerly traded their valuables for them.

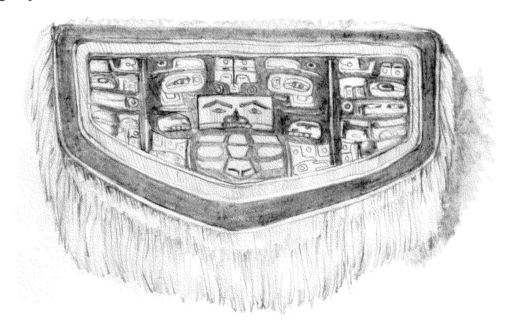

# Make a Chilkat Blanket

**Materials:**
• individual copies of the pattern on the page 21.
• pencil, markers or crayons
• scissors

**Directions:**
1. Explain to your class what a mirror image is.
2. Model at the board or on an overhead projector beginning at the top in the middle. Repeat the pattern on the left. Work together until students understand the concept.
3. Color in one section and its reverse as it is finished.
4. Use yellow, blue, and black, leaving the background plain to indicate the off-white natural color.
5. Cut on the dotted line.
6. Add fringe by cutting narrow slits in the plain border.

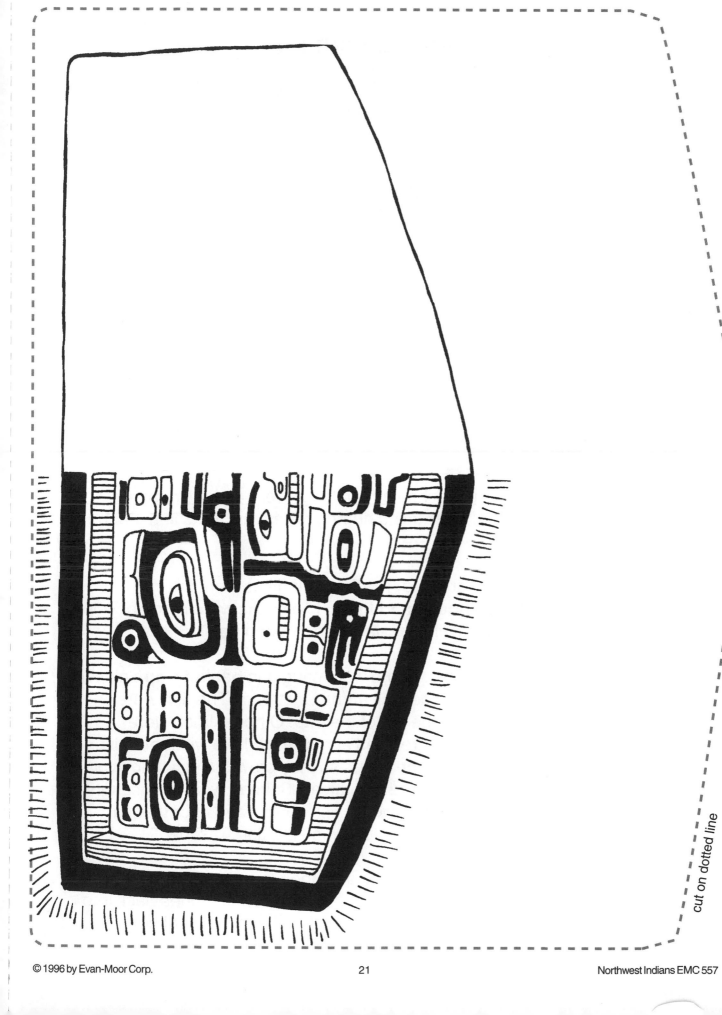

cut on dotted line

21

# Fish and Fishing

Catching fish was an art.

Near the shore, small fish (eulachon and herring) were caught in **dip nets**, net bags hung from a pole, or by using herring **rakes**, big forks that stabbed the fish.

To catch larger fish (halibut and cod) Northwest Indians went out into the ocean in canoes and used **hooks and lines**. The hooks were made of wood or bone and were attached to lines fastened to wooden poles.

Salmon were caught three ways. Some were caught in **basket traps** placed in narrow openings in a pole fence built across a stream. The fish were speared through an opening in the top of the trap. Other salmon were caught in **weirs**, latticed fences stretched across the whole width of a river. The salmon could not swim over the weirs, so they crowded just below the surface where they could be speared by natives. Salmon were also caught in **stone traps** built across streams so that fish could swim over them at high tide but were trapped behind the wall when the tide was low.

The natives believed that the salmon gave up their lives to feed them. To make it possible for the salmon to live again, they threw its bones back into the sea. To this day, families do this ceremonially with the first salmon caught each year.

 Northwest Indians EMC 557

# Catch a Fish!

**Directions:**
1. Below are pictures of the various ways fish were caught.
2. For each picture write the name of a fish caught in this way.
3. Names in the word box will help you.
4. You may use a name more than once.

| cod | eulachon | halibut | herring | salmon |
|-----|----------|---------|---------|--------|

**dip net**

**hook and line**

**rake**

**basket trap**

**spear**

**weir**

# Fishing and Food

Northwest Coast natives were never hungry. The dense forests provided meat. Bows and arrows felled deer, elk, and mountain goat. Baited traps caught wolves and bears. However, it was much easier to get food from the beaches, streams, rivers, and ocean.

Clams, oysters, octopuses, crabs, mussels, eelgrass, and seaweed could all be found on the beaches. Salmon, herring, eulachon, and dogfish swam in the rivers and streams. Porpoises, seals, codfish, halibut, sea lions, and sea otters lived in the ocean. Sea birds and water fowl flew in the sky and the eggs of gulls, puffins, and other birds could be gathered from their nests.

The prize catch of all was the whale. Weighing about 1,500 pounds, one bull whale could feed a whole village for many days. The Nootka and Makah hunted them far out into the ocean. Other tribes looked for dead whales that washed up on their beaches.

There were three basic ways of cooking their food: grilling over an open fire, baking in a pit oven heated with hot rocks, and boiling in a big box filled with water that was heated with hot stones.

Fish stew was the main meal. Sometimes fish was eaten raw, other times uncooked but soaked in oil from cod, herring, eulachon, dogfish, shark, or whales. Northwest Coast natives loved oil. A special delicacy was raspberries or strawberries beaten up with fish oil.

Enough food was gathered during the summer months and preserved by drying or smoking to last the rest of the year.

**Discussion questions:**
How do we preserve food today?
Do we use any of the ways of preserving food that the Indians did?
Do we cook food in any of the ways they did?
Do we eat any of the same types of food?

# Canoes

Although canoes came in many sizes, they were constructed in similar ways.

The largest canoe was 60' (18 m) long and 8' (2.5 m) wide made from a large tree cut down with stone hammers and chisels. The limbs were removed and the tree was hollowed using a chisel and maul. The outside was finished with another simple tool, the adz. The hollowed trunk was then filled with heated water to soften the wood so that crosspieces could be forced in to help the canoe keep its shape. The outside was blackened by charring and then oiled.

A whaling canoe might be painted red, black, blue-green, and yellow; often with a killer whale design on its bow. A war canoe was decorated yellow, white, or black, and often had an animal carved on the bow.

In the early days paddles were used to propel the canoes. Later the white man's sails, woven from bark fiber, were adopted.

The largest canoes could hold at least thirty people. Paddled by slaves, these were used for long voyages to potlatches or for warfare. Smaller canoes carried people on shorter trips or up rivers and inlets to hunt or fish. These canoes were not usually decorated. Sometimes a canoe even served as a coffin, set on a scaffold high up in a tree.

See the size of a large canoe by marking off a section of your school hallway or playground 60' (18 m) x 8' (2.5 m). See how many students can fit in it, sitting cross-legged or kneeling.

 Northwest Indians EMC 557

# Handy Units of Measure

When Indians made their canoes they had no measuring devices such as meter sticks, protractors, or compasses. They used something they always had with them—parts of their bodies.

**Directions:**
Complete the chart by using parts of your body to measure things in your classroom.

| What body part did you use? | What did you measure? | What size did it measure? |
|---|---|---|
| elbow to wrist | *desk top* | *2 x 1.5 measures* |
| tip of thumb to 1st joint | | |
| finger tip to elbow | | |
| shoulder to wrist | | |
| knee to ankle | | |
| length of foot | | |
| one stride | | |
| wrist to fingertips | | |
| outstretched hand thumb to little finger | | |

Make up your own unit of measurement here:

| | | |
|---|---|---|
| | | |

 Northwest Indians EMC 557

# The White Sea Bird

For hundreds of years the people of the Northwest Pacific Coast lived the way their ancestors did. They sailed their canoes along the coast, but they knew nothing of the rest of the world.

Then in 1519, a villager, looking out to the sea, saw what looked like a giant bird flying close to the water. It was much like a gull, but its wings were huge.

They called it a "white seabird" and watched as it headed toward their shore. As it came closer they saw it was a giant canoe, and the creatures who sailed it had reddish-white skin. It was the sailing ship of English Captain Francis Drake on his search for a sea route through North America.

To the natives, it remained a giant white sea bird, and stories about it were told from generation to generation.

Pretend you were one of the natives who saw the sailing ship for the first time. What might you have thought it was? How would you have described it?

In the space below, draw a cartoon of two natives seeing the ship for the first time. Write a caption below the picture.

# Whaling

All Northwest Coastal men fished, but whale hunting was done only by the Nootka and Makah village chiefs. The village chief was the only one who could afford the crew and the large sea-worthy canoes. Hunters were hired and trained by the chief. This was a dangerous job. Natives respected the whale and believed human effort alone was not enough to subdue one. Therefore, the whole whale hunt, from beginning to end, had to follow rigid rules. If anything was done wrong, the hunt was destined to be difficult or unsuccessful.

Whales were never killed quickly. Harpoons that were thrown had floats of inflated fish bladders attached to them to slow the whale's movement and keep it from sinking. A whale weighing up to forty tons might tow the canoes around for three or four days before tiring. Once the whale was exhausted, the men slashed the tendons of its tail and drove a lance into its heart. The dead whale was towed to shore.

When the hunters reached the beach, the whole village celebrated. All parts of the whale were used. Flesh and skin were eaten. The intestines were made into containers for oil. The sinew was made into ropes and lines. Blubber not eaten was turned into oil.

Catching a whale was important for two reasons. It supplied the village with food and raw materials. It also proved that the chief and his people were properly attuned to the spirits of nature.

 Northwest Indians EMC 557

# Make a Flow Chart of a Whale Hunt

**Directions:**

A flow chart is a diagram showing the order in which events happen. This flow chart is missing information. Fill in the blanks with events that could possibly happen next.

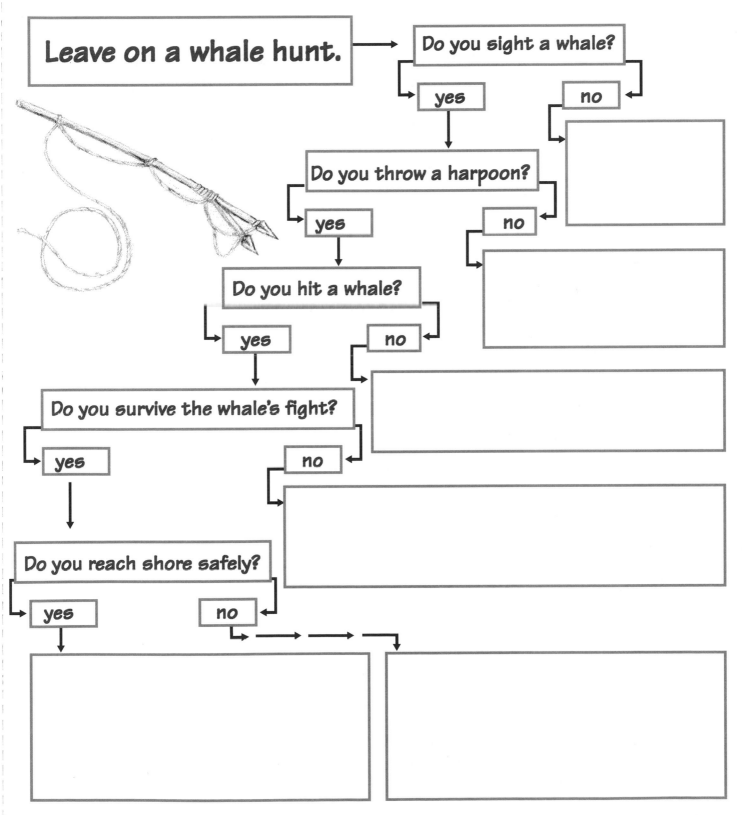

# Tools

Northwest Coast Indians made their tools from materials they could find.

Hand-held stone hammers and wooden wedges were used to split logs into boards.

The adze was a small cutting tool, with the blade made from a sharpened hard, flat stone. Adzes were used for cutting, scraping, and gouging.

The awl, made from hard wood, thorns, or a bone splinter, was a pointed tool used to punch holes. Drills, made from sharp bone fastened to a wooden shaft, were rotated between the palms of the hands to make holes in tougher materials.

Chisels—sharpened pieces of horn or a stone set in a wooden shaft—were used to carve wood.

Bark beaters and mauls were used to soften and shred cedar bark so it could be used for weaving. Bark beaters had handles and were made of whale bones that had long grooves in them. Mauls were made of heavy stone with a round, blunt end

With these simple tools, the Northwest natives made both useful and beautiful objects from wood.

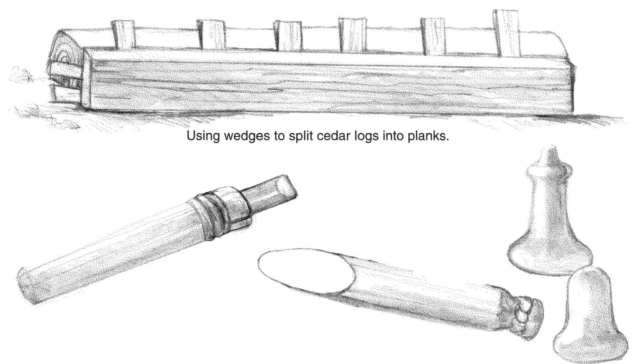

Using wedges to split cedar logs into planks.

# Tools

**Directions:**
From the descriptions of tools used by Northwest Coast natives, match the tools pictured with the names in the word box. On the lines below each name write one task that tool might have been used for.

| | | | | | |
|---|---|---|---|---|---|
| adze | bark beater | chisel | hammer | drill | maul |

tool: _____    tool: _____
use: _____    use: _____

tool: _____    tool: _____
use: _____    use: _____

tool: _____    tool: _____
use: _____    use: _____

# Woodworking

Northwest Natives had ample leisure time to pursue their arts. They made beautiful carved and painted wooden objects: totem poles, clubs, paddles, headdresses, masks, dishes fish hooks rattles, and gambling sticks.

Handsomely carved wooden screens separated sleeping quarters of high class families. Dolls and toy canoes were fashioned from wood, too.

Some of the most intricately carved items were masks worn by ceremonial dancers. These represented human faces, birds and animals. Hinges and strings let the masks open to reveal the faces inside.

Large cedar wood storage boxes were made of one long plank that was grooved, then steamed until it was soft enough to bend into a four-sided box. When the open sides and the bottom were fastened with wooden pegs or sewed with spruce roots, the boxes were so watertight that they could be filled with water and hot stones and used to cook food. The boxes were decorated with carvings and paintings on the front and sides.

All these wondrous works of art were carved with just a few simple tools.

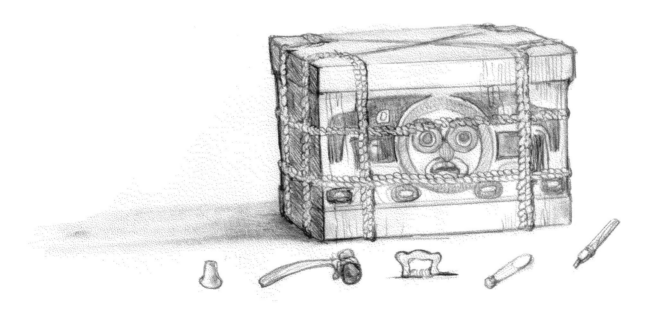

# Build a Box

These decorated cardboard boxes are fun to make and show how the natives made boxes from single grooved pieces.

**Materials for each box:**
- cardboard piece 2' x 1' (61 cm x 30.5 cm)
- scissors
- markers or tempera paint
- glue or clear tape

**Directions:**
1. Cut cardboard on solid lines as shown.
2. Score each piece on the dotted lines.
3. Fold on scores and tape or glue sides and bottom to form a box.
4. Decorate sides with designs of birds or animals.

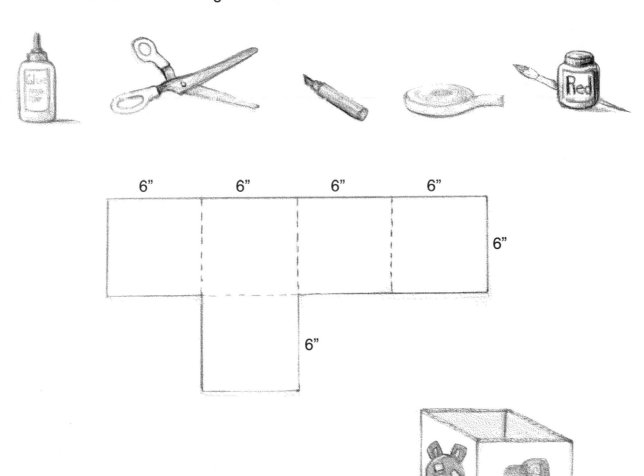

# Art

Like all Native Americans, the Haida, the Tlingit, and the Kwakiutl drew the birds, animals, and people around them. Realistic details were exaggerated. For example the beaver is shown with two extremely large front teeth and a big tail; the raven has a very long beak and unusually wide wings; the whale has an unnaturally wide mouth and a huge dorsal fin.

Two shapes that are often seen in painting and weaving are an egg shape and the symbol U. Parts of animals like an eye, a claw, a tail, or a mouth are put in these shapes. Eyes were thought to have magical qualities, so they were used to fill in any empty spaces. No space was left blank.

**Directions:**
The Northwest Coast natives carved from wood. Your students will enjoy creating their own sculptures shaped from clay.

Brainstorm to come up with a list of birds, animals, or fish native to the Northwest coast. Discuss the features of each animal that might be exaggerated in the sculpture. For example: the eyes of an owl; the teeth of a wolf.

# Where Did the Colors Come From?

Northwest coastal artists did a lot of carving that was painted. Paint brushes were made from fine cedar bark strands or from porcupine fur. Their paints were limited to colors found in nature.

Below are listed both the materials they used and the colors they made. Match each color with the correct material by writing the number of the color on the line. You may use a number more than once. Look up any words you do not know.

Hint: Picture each material in your mind. What color is it? If squeezed or rubbed, what color do you think would result?

1. black

2. brown

3. red

4. green

5. purple

6. white

7. yellow

_____ berries

_____ dark berries

_____ decayed fungus

_____ charcoal

_____ flakes from copper-bearing rocks

_____ animal blood

_____ clay

_____ bear dung mixed with chewed cedar

_____ graphite

_____ ocher

Many weavers today make their own dyes to color their yarn. They use things like berries, onions, leaves, and flowers. Can you find something in nature that would make a good color for you to paint a design with?

# Totem Poles

One of the most well-recognized symbols of the Northwest Coast is the totem pole. Totem poles were not religious symbols. They were status symbols, and only the very wealthy could afford them.

The natives told stories by carving totems on poles. The totems were animals that native families believed were their ancestors, and from whom they got their clan names. Each part of a totem pole had a definite meaning, and together they told a specific story.

There were many kinds of poles. Some were house posts supporting the roof, often honoring a deceased chief. Others memorialized a dead person or served to hold his remains. Finally, there were poles carved to ridicule someone or shame him. These figures were carved upside down.

The wet climate has ruined old totem poles, so there is no accurate record of how long ago they were first used. Originally they were carved with knives and adzes. After the Europeans came, the natives had access to metal tools and could build larger poles with more intricate carvings. White missionaries thought the carvings were religious, so they had them chopped down and used for firewood.

# Make a Totem Pole

A class totem pole is fun to make and can honor your class as a "clan" or "family." Make your pole as tall as space permits. You may need to make two or more.

Brainstorm and list Northwest animals and the qualities each might exemplify. For example: bear–great strength; eagle–keen vision. Each student will choose an animal with whom they share qualities and make his/her own animal symbol.

Remind students that carved figures were symbolic rather than realistic. Eyes were always big. Teeth, beaks, wings, and snouts were also exaggerated.

## Materials
- 9" x 12" (23 x 30.5 cm) gray construction paper
- scraps of construction paper in colors of black, brown, red, green, purple, white and yellow
- markers or paint
- scissors
- glue
- tape
- push pins

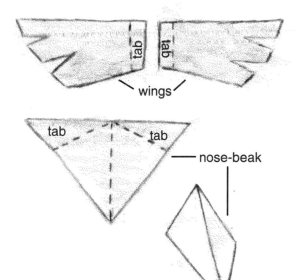

## Directions:
1. Fold under 1" (2.5 cm) along the long sides of the gray construction paper. The folds will be on the right and left sides of the figure.
2. Create the animal by coloring or by cutting and pasting construction paper shapes onto the gray paper. The background can remain gray to look like weathered wood.
3. To make 3-D features for the beak, teeth or claws, draw on seperate pieces of construction paper. Cut out the features, fold tabs, and then glue the tabs onto your design.
5. Attach students' animals together by taping the back sides of the top and bottom edges.
6. Bend the long sides to give a round, 3-D appearance. Attach to a bulletin board by pushing pins through the folded 1" (2.5 cm) edge.

37                Northwest Indians EMC 557

# Potlatch

The word "potlatch" is a Nootka word meaning "party." It was a way for a chief to show off his wealth by giving everything away.

Potlatches were given to celebrate important events such as births, marriages, the raising of totem poles, and passing along an inheritance.

Strict rules governed potlatches. Invitations were sent out far ahead of time. Months were spent getting food and gifts ready for the many guests. Dances and songs had to be practiced, costumes and masks prepared, speeches and ceremonials perfected, and seating order assigned. Everything had to be just right.

Guests dressed in their finest outfits and arrived in war canoes. They were welcomed on the beach with singing and speeches, then escorted to the chief's lodge. Days of feasting followed. Guests ate fish stew and other delicacies. Singers and dancers performed myths and family legends. Then gifts were distributed by the host. The greatest gifts went to the highest ranking guests and on down until everyone received something. The gifts included coppers, canoes, blankets, boxes, furs, dentalium shells, and even slaves.

The host might give away so much that he would make himself poor. His riches would be replenished later when it was his turn to be the guest at some other chief's potlatch.

Have students imagine they are attending a potlatch. Assign them their own "ranks." Have another group pretend to be a TV crew covering the affair for a national network. Describe the setting, the activities, and the gifts. Be sure to include interviews with the chief and some of the guests.

# Music

Singing and dancing was popular among Northwest Coast natives.

Often women sang while men played instruments. An empty chest hung from a house beam served as a drum when it was struck with a cedar-bound stick. A drum-like sound was also made by striking the roof boards of the house with long poles. Planks placed on two wooden blocks and struck by wooden sticks was still another kind of drum.

Tambourines were made from rawhide stretched over a hoop. Sometimes simple rattles were attached to them; other times they were struck with the hand.

Whistles were carved from hollowed-out sticks of wood. Simple rattles were made by tying deer hooves to long sticks and shaking them up and down.

The most beautiful instruments were wooden rattles that were painstakingly carved to resemble human or animal shapes. Inside were placed pebbles or shells. These were struck against the hand.

An instrument every native always had with him —his hands— clapped in rhythm to accompanying tunes.

Although their music was not always melodious, it certainly was loud and spirited.

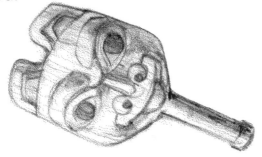 

Students can make their own simple instruments.
- Balance a board between two boxes or chairs. Use hands, rulers or pencils to beat on the part of the board that is not resting on the bases.
- Suspend a heavy cardboard box from a meter stick that is taped between two desks. Strike the box with a ruler or pencil.
- Stretch a piece of heavy plastic sheeting (or a plastic bag) on an embroidery hoop. Strike it with a pencil or hand.

# Mythology

As long as people have lived on earth they have explained things they did not understand through myths about supernatural beings. To the natives of the Northwest Coast, one of the most important beings is Raven, the trickster credited with forming the lakes, rivers, streams, and the sun, moon, and stars.

The following story tells how Raven made the tides:

The ocean level had been very high for a very long time. The people were very hungry because they could not reach the sea plants and animals that were all hidden under the deep water.

Raven decided to change the situation, so he flew to the home of the old lady who held the tide line in her hands. Knowing she would not willingly let go, Raven thought of a way to trick her. He sat down beside her and told about some delicious clams he had just eaten. Now, the old woman knew there were no clams within reach, so she questioned him. When Raven insisted they were very easy to get, the old woman went to her doorway to see for herself. When she did this, Raven gave her a push, then blinded her by throwing sand in her eyes. As she fell, she let go of the tide line.

Immediately the tide went out, leaving clams and crabs and all sorts of seafood on the beach. Raven ate and ate and ate. So did all the people, thanking Raven as they did.

Returning to the old woman's home, Raven agreed to give back her sight if she promised to let go of the tide line twice each day. From then on, the people were never hungry, and to this day the tide comes in and goes out every day.

# Write a Myth

In all the stories Raven used trickery to make things happen. One way he did this was by changing himself into whatever plant, animal, person, or object he chose. He turned himself into an old man to steal salmon from the beavers; a shiny, dark, green leaf to steal the sun from the fisherman's daughter; a duck to catch halibut; and a deer to steal fire.

If you were Raven, what would you turn yourself into?

**Directions:**

1. Chose something for Raven to steal that people need:

   _____

2. Your title will be:

   **"How Raven Stole**_____**"**

3. Choose a character (animal or human) for Raven to steal from:

   _____

   Will this character be good or bad? _____

   Two reasons why it is good or bad: _____

   _____.

4. What thing will Raven turn himself into in order to steal?_____

   _____.

   Give two reasons why it good or bad: _____

   _____.

5. Will Raven be successful in stealing what he wants? _____.

6. Two outcomes that happen as a result of Raven succedding or not:

   _____

   _____

   _____

Using the details you have just filled in, write your own "Raven" myth. Write your first draft on lined paper. Meet with a friend to share your myths. Help each other to make your myths even better. Write your final copy on the form your teacher provides.

Note: Reproduce this form for students to write their Raven myths (Page 41).

Title: ____________________

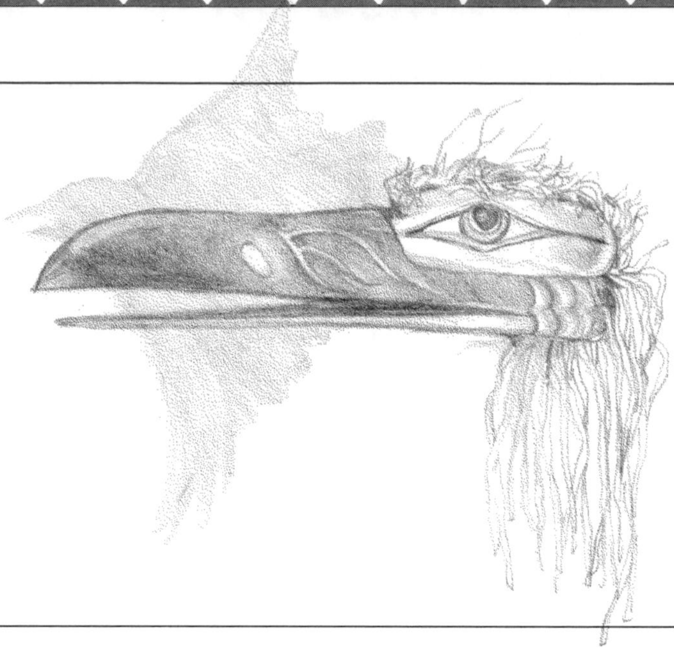

# Tillikum

Tillikum means "friend" and is a game that has been played by the Indian children of the Northwest coast for a long time. It resembles a Japanese game and probably came from Asia.

The game uses three symbols for **water**, **earth**, and **fire**. Using one hand, this is how the symbols are made:

• **earth** - hand held out flat with palm down
• **water** - hand held out with fingers and thumb hanging down
• **fire** - fingers and thumb point up with palm facing forward

**To play:**
• Stand facing a partner.
• Raise one hand made into a fist up to your shoulder.
• Do this three times together counting: one, two, three.
• On the count of three, each person makes a symbol for either earth, water, or fire

**A point is scored when:**

• **earth** drinks the **water**
• **water** puts out the **fire**
• **fire** scorches the **earth**

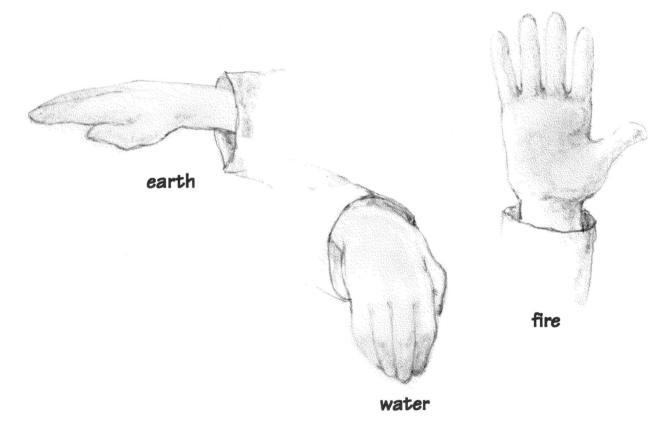

earth

water

fire

# Name the Tribes

**Tlingit**, **Haida**, **Tsimshian**, **Bella Bella**, **Kwakiutl**, **Nootka** and **Makah** are names of some of the native tribes who lived on the Northwest Coast of America.

Each word square below contains the name of one tribe. To find it, you must connect the letters in order without skipping spaces. You may go up, down or diagonal. Some letters will not be used at all. When you have found the name, write it below the square.

Example: To find the word "tribe" in this square, begin with circled letter and follow the arrows.

```
B    R    B
E    I    R
I    T    E
```
Name: t r i b e

**Square 1**
```
D   A   A
H   I   A
D   A   D
```
Name: _ _ _ _ _

**1**

**Square 2**
```
L   T   W   K
U   K   A   I
I   K   I   W
L   T   U   T
```
Name: _ _ _ _ _ _ _ _

**2**

**Square 3**
```
N   A   O   A
K   O   A   T
A   T   K   T
O   A   K   O
```
Name: _ _ _ _ _ _ _

**3**

**Square 4**
```
L   L   A   B
L   E   E   A
A   B   E   L
E   L   A   L
```
Name: _ _ _ _ _

_ _ _ _ _

**4**

**Square 5**
```
T   I   G   N
L   T   L   T
N   I   G   T
G   G   I   N
```
Name: _ _ _ _ _ _ _

**5**

**Square 6**
```
N   T   H   N
N   I   A   I
S   M   S   K
T   H   A   I
```
Name: _ _ _ _ _

**6**

**Square 7**
```
N   T   A   N
N   I   S   I
S   M   S   H
T   N   A   I
```
Name: _ _ _ _ _ _ _ _ _

**7**

Northwest Indians EMC 557

# Review Game: Categories

**Directions:**
1. Three words in each list belong together.
2. One word in each list does not belong.
3. Cross out the word that does not belong.
4. On the line at the right, write a category that the remaining three words are all part of.
5. You may choose categories from the box at the bottom of the page.

| word list | category |
|---|---|
| 1. bay   sound   gulf   canal | _____ |
| 2. sea otter   seal   eagle   bear | _____ |
| 3. democratic   aristocratic   lavish   excessive | _____ |
| 4. herring   salmon   eulachon   angelfish | _____ |
| 5. religion   status symbol   legend   memorial | _____ |
| 6. drying   smoking   toasting   boiling | _____ |
| 7. whale   mountain goat   elk   reindeer | _____ |
| 8. berries   eulachon   fungus   charcoal | _____ |
| 9. carving   weaving   etching   painting | _____ |
| 10. hats   sandals   capes   baskets | _____ |
| 11. adze   saw   chisel   hammer | _____ |
| 12. nobles   chiefs   commoners   ambassadors | _____ |
| 13. lace   dentalium   copper   blankets | _____ |
| 14. sarong   skirt   moccasins   tunic | _____ |
| 15. berries   olives   salmon   seaweed | _____ |
| 16. Tlingit   Nootka   Tsimshian   Nez Perce | _____ |

## Category Box

animals used for fur
bodies of water
characteristics of NW Coast Society
classes of society
clothing worn by women
foods eaten by NW Natives
materials used to make paint
NW Coast animals

NW Coast art forms
NW fish
NW Coast tribes
reasons for totem poles
things that were woven
things used for exchange
tools used by NW Coast Natives
ways to preserve food

Northwest Indians EMC 557

# Crossword Review

**Word Box**

adze
archipelago
canoe
cedar
chief
cod
deer
drum
lodge
maritime
mask
maul
net
oil
potlatch
salmon
sea
totem
whale

**Across:**
4. "The" tree for NW natives
6. location on or near the sea
8. carved stone used as a hammer
9. woven device for catching fish
10. covering to disguise face
11. large sea mammal
13. ocean fish
15. fish that returns to streams to spawn
16. another name for plank house
17. head person in the village

**Down:**
1. hand-held scraping tool
2. musical instrument played by striking
3. huge ceremonial feast
4. large chain of islands
7. carved animal symbol
12. greasy liquid obtained from animals
13. boat with pointed ends
14. forest animal with antlers
15. large body of water

Northwest Indians EMC 557

# Northwest Coastal Natives Today

In two hundred years explorers, traders, settlers, missionaries, and white governments have almost erased the centuries old way of life for the Northwest Coast Natives. White diseases depleted the native population. Native languages and ceremonies were outlawed. Totem poles were chopped down and burned. Children were taught to be ashamed of their culture and encouraged to act like whites. White laws took of hunting and fishing lands from the natives who had always used them.

Over the last fifty years foreign fishing fleets have been competing with local fishing, forcing many native fishermen to find employment in the cities. Poverty is increasing in many of the villages.

However, recent emphasis on education has led to many natives entering skilled and professional occupations. Some are lawyers and doctors, even more teachers and artists. With education has also come a demand to have equal rights under the law.

Today Northwest Natives are growing in numbers. Also growing is pride in their heritage and the desire to work for its preservation. More and more, Indians are trying to find a way to retain valuable aspects of their ancestry and also live in the modern world.

And, as the "outside" world becomes more environmentally aware, it is coming to appreciate and adopt the native ways of preserving natural resources.

# Ecology - Then and Now

The Northwest Coast natives hunted and fished for food and used the resources of the forest for clothing and shelter. Like native groups all over North America, they believed that the earth's resources were a gift and must never be used carelessly or wastefully. They never killed an animal for sport. If an animal was killed, all parts of it were used. They never felled a tree unless they had a use for it, and they found uses for all its parts.

Their extreme care of nature was partly due to religious beliefs that every animal had a spirit and could return to earth to help or harm the person who had killed it. The natives talked to the animals and held ceremonies to please or thank them. They were also conscious that earth's resources should be used wisely so they would never be used up.

Today there is a great effort in our country to eliminate waste, stop pollution of water and air, and practice the 3 R's of Reduce, Reuse, and Recycle. Many of our methods of doing this are new and modern. Many others, though, were practiced by natives for centuries.

Use a Venn diagram to show how old and new overlap by drawing two big interlocking circles on your bulletin board or chalkboard. Have students name ecology practices that were true only of early natives, and write those in the first circle part. Have them name practices that are new today. Write them in the last circle part. Use the middle circle part to list practices that are common to both groups.

**Example:**